Animal Young

Amphibians

Rod Theodorou

Heinemann
LIBRARY

First published in Great Britain by
Heinemann Library,
Halley Court, Jordan Hill, Oxford OX2 8EJ
a division of Reed Educational and Professional
Publishing Ltd.
Heinemann is a registered trademark of Reed
Educational & Professional Publishing Ltd.

OXFORD MELBOURNE AUCKLAND
JOHANNESBURG BLANTYRE GABORONE
IBADAN PORTSMOUTH (NH) USA CHICAGO

Designed by Celia Floyd
Illustrations by Alan Fraser
Printed in Hong Kong/China

03 02 01 00 99
10 9 8 7 6 5 4 3 2 1

ISBN 0 431 03072 3

British Library Cataloguing in Publication Data

Theodorou, Rod
  Amphibians. – (Animal young)
1. Amphibians – Infancy – Juvenile literature
I. Title
597.8'139

Acknowledgements

The Publishers would like to thank the following for
permission to reproduce photographs:

BBC: Dietmar Hill p. 10; Bruce Coleman: Robert
Maier p. 7, Jane Burton pp. 15, 25, Phil Savoie p. 17;
FLPA: Chris Mattison p. 9, Tony Wharton p. 18, John
Watkins p. 23; Michael & Patricia Fogden pp. 5, 13;
NHPA: Jean-Lois Le Moigne p. 11, Karl Switak pp. 12,
22; OSF: Richard K La Val p. 6, Ian West p, 8, G I
Bernard pp 14, 16, 21, J A L Cooke, p. 24; Planet
Earth: John & Gillian Lythgoe p. 14: Tony Stone:
Robin Smith p. 20.

Cover photograph reproduced with permission of
Oxford Scientific Films/G I Bernard

Every effort has been made to contact copyright
holders of any material reproduced in this book.
Any omissions will be rectified in subsequent
printings if notice is given to the Publisher.

Any words appearing in the text in bold, **like this**,
are explained in the Glossary.

Contents

Introduction

There are many different kinds of animals. All animals have babies. They look after their babies in different ways.

These are the six main animal groups.

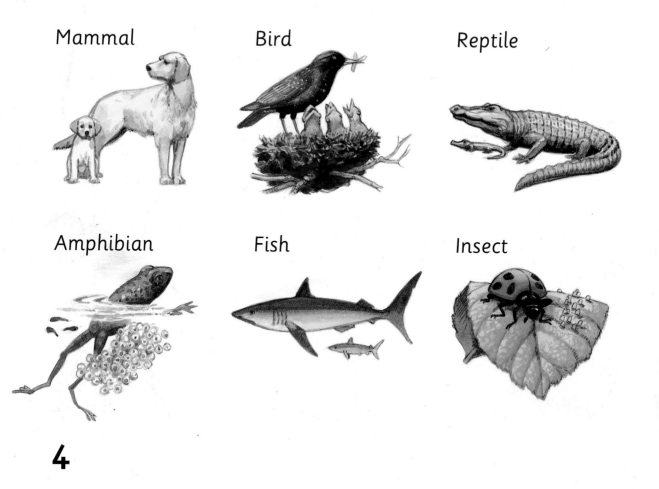

Mammal

Bird

Reptile

Amphibian

Fish

Insect

This book is about amphibians. Amphibians can live on land and in water. The young often look very different to their parents.

This is an adult frog next to its young.

what is an amphibian?

All adult amphibians:
- breathe air
- have soft, **moist** skin
- eat other animals.

glass frog

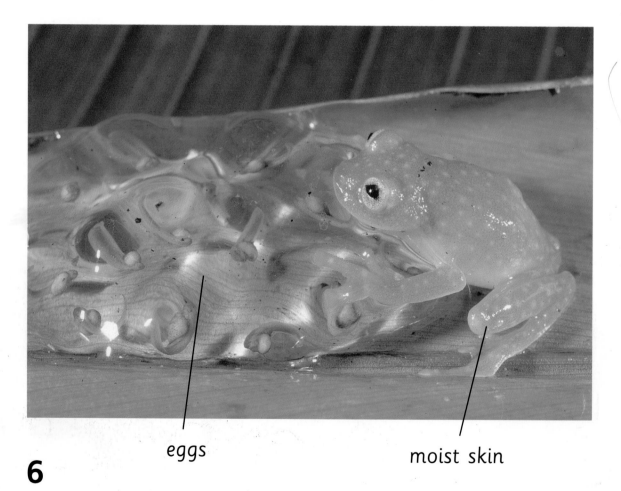

eggs

moist skin

Most amphibians:

- live in fresh water, or near it on land
- lay eggs that their young **hatch** from
- have four legs to help them move
- have a good **sense** of smell, even under water.

This spotted salamander's skin will stay moist, even if it is not in water.

Laying eggs

Amphibians **mate** in or near water. Most females lay jelly-covered eggs in the water. The jelly protects the eggs. They grow very quickly.

These jelly-covered frog eggs are called frogspawn.

The eggs are often eaten by other animals. The females lay lots of eggs so that some of the young will live.

The female painted frog can lay up to 1000 eggs at once.

Looking after the eggs

Some amphibians try to lay their eggs in places other hungry animals will not find them. They lay their eggs under stones or fix them to plants.

The smooth newt uses its back legs to fix its eggs to water plants.

Amphibians that live and **mate** on land cannot hide their eggs in water. They have to take special care of their eggs.

The male midwife toad carries the female's eggs around with him until they are ready to **hatch**.

Hatching eggs

Some amphibian eggs are ready to **hatch** only 24 hours after they have been laid. Others can take much longer to hatch.

The two-toed amphiuma stays coiled around her eggs for five months until they hatch!

When the eggs hatch, **larvae** come out of them. Some amphibian larvae look like their parents, but most look very different. They have **gills** to help them breathe underwater.

Frog and toad larvae are called tadpoles.

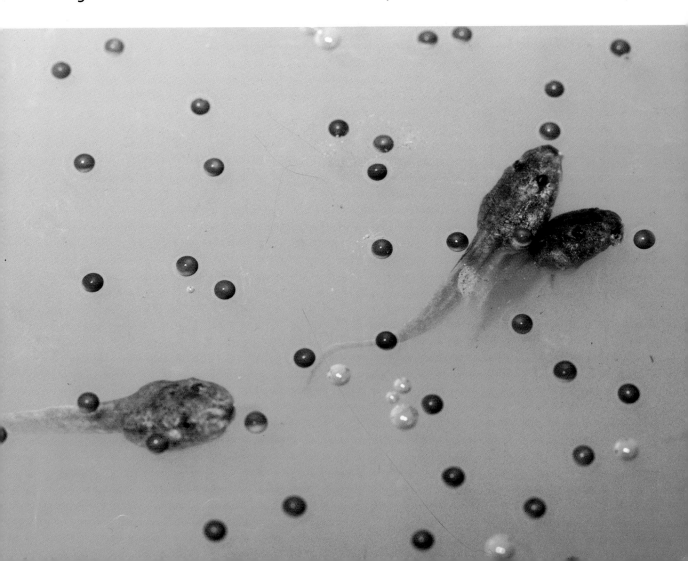

Finding food

Amphibian **larvae** are always hungry. They need to eat lots of food to help them grow. Larvae that hatch from eggs eat the **yolk** from their egg first.

These tadpoles are eating their first meal.

14

Soon the larvae have to find their own food. Most larvae do not eat animals. They eat plants and **algae** that they suck into their mouths.

Salamander larvae are unusual because they eat other animals, like small insects.

Staying safe

Newly **hatched** amphibian **larvae** cannot move very fast. They are easy for **predators** to catch and eat. Water insects, fish and other amphibians will attack the larvae.

This dragonfly **nymph** has caught a tadpole.

Some amphibians lay their eggs in tiny ponds or puddles where predators will not find their larvae. A few even stand guard over their eggs until they hatch.

This glass frog is guarding its eggs.

Live young

Some amphibians do not lay eggs. They give birth to live young. Their young are born with legs, ready to swim and feed. Some are even born on land.

Alpine salamanders give birth on land to just one or two live young.

Amphibians that give birth to live young usually live in places where it would be difficult to lay eggs.

This salamander gives birth to live young. It lives in streams. If it laid eggs they would be washed away by the water.

Amazing changes

Amphibian **larvae** that live in water change. As they get bigger they grow legs. The **gills** disappear. Soon they are ready to crawl out of the water and live on land.

These frog tadpoles have grown their back legs.

20

Frog and toad tadpoles lose their tails as their bodies change. Newt and salamander larvae keep their tails. The skin may also become more colourful.

The tail of this young frog has nearly disappeared.

Living on land

Many plant-eating **larvae** change into meat-eating adults. Once they begin their life on land they start to hunt other animals to eat. They may eat worms, spiders, and small animals.

This huge African bullfrog will eat mice, other frogs, and even snakes!

Some amphibian young stay near the ponds or streams in which they were born. Others wander off and spend their lives on the land.

Young frogs like wet weather. It is easier for them to move on wet ground.

Amazing amphibians

Some kinds of amphibian look very different to frogs, toads, newts or salamanders. They are shaped more like eels or worms and live underwater or underground.

The caecilian lives more like a worm. Some live underground and lay their eggs in a burrow.

Other kinds of amphibian look like large **larvae**, but their bodies never change. They spend all their lives in the water and never come on to land.

This axolotl is an amphibian that looks like a larva all its life.

Growing up

This is how a frog **larva** grows up.
The larva does not look like its parents.

Growth of a frog

1 The adult female lays her eggs.

2 The tadpoles **hatch** from the eggs. They eat the egg jelly.

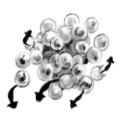

3 The tadpoles eat lots of food. They get bigger and bigger.

4 The tadpoles grow legs.

5 The young frogs crawl onto land.

This is how a newt larva grows up.
The larva looks a lot like its parents.

Growth of a newt

1 The adult female lays her eggs and wraps each one in weeds.

 2 The tiny larvae hatch from the eggs.

3 The larvae eat lots of food. They get bigger and bigger. They already have tiny legs.

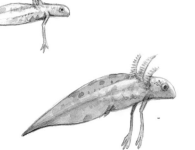

4 The larvae's legs grow bigger.

5 The young newt is fully grown.

Amphibians and other animals

		Fish
What they look like:	Bones inside body	all
	Number of legs	none
	Hair on body	none
	Scaly skin	most
	Wings	none
	Feathers	none
Where they live:	Lives on land	none
	Lives in water	all
How they are born:	Grows babies inside body	some
	Lays eggs	most
How they feed young:	Feeds baby milk	none
	Bring babies food	none

	Amphibians	Insects	Reptiles	Birds	Mammals
	all	none	all	all	all
	4 or none	6	4 or none	2	2 or 4
	none	all	none	none	all
	none	none	all	none	few
	none	most	none	all	some
	none	none	none	all	none
	most	most	most	all	most
	some	some	some	none	some
	few	some	some	none	most
	most	most	most	all	few
	none	none	none	none	all
	none	none	none	most	most

Glossary

algae   very small plants that grow in water or damp places

coiled   to be wrapped around in a circle

gill   part of an amphibian or fish's body that takes oxygen from water to help it breathe

hatch   to be born from an egg

larva   (more than one = larvae) animal baby that hatches from an egg but looks different to an adult

mate   when a male and a female animal come together to make babies

moist   something that is a little bit wet

nymph   a young insect that looks very like an adult insect when it is born

predator   an animal that hunts and kills other animals for food

sense   to be able to feel, see, smell, hear or taste something

yolk   part of an egg that is food for a baby animal

Further reading

Amazing Frogs and Toads, Barry Clarke, *Amazing Worlds*, Dorling Kindersley, 1990.

Amphibian, Dr Barry Clarke, *Eyewitness Guides*, Dorling Kindersley, 1993.

Frog, Kim Taylor and Jane Burton, *See How They Grow*, Dorling Kindersley, 1991.

Life cycle of a Frog, Angela Royston, Heinemann Library, 1998.

Tadpole and Frog, Christine Black and Barrie Watts, *Stopwatch Books*, A and C Black, 1984.

The Frog and The Toad, Mike Linley, *Junior Survival Library*, Boxtree Ltd, 1990.

The Tadpole, *Nature Close Ups*, Raintree Publishers, 1986.

Index